Puffin Books
Editor: Kaye Webb

Once There Was a Boy
and Other Stories

Once there was a boy who liked pulling pigtails, another
boy who couldn't remember his own address, a silly king
who wanted a bell tower but was much too grand to
put up with the building noises, a shy man who wore
different coloured socks every day, and lots of other
equally charming, interesting and funny characters, all of
them invented by Malcolm Carrick who has a gift for
keeping us guessing and gasping. It is one of the rules in
all his stories that one strange thing leads to another, but
they are all great fun and so are the action rhymes and
jingles that give a breathing space between these
imaginative stories.

Malcolm Carrick has interests in playgroups, adventure
playgroups, and music for under-fives, and his acquain-
tance with children of this age gives his stories a
special value. Some of the stories and rhymes in this
book have been used in BBC Play School.

For children of four years upwards.

Once There Was a Boy

and Other Stories

Malcolm Carrick

Illustrated by Barbara Walker

 Puffin Books

Puffin Books, Penguin Books Ltd, Harmondsworth,
Middlesex, England
Penguin Books Inc., 7110 Ambassador Road,
Baltimore, Maryland 21207, U.S.A.
Penguin Books Australia Ltd, Ringwood,
Victoria, Australia
Penguin Books Canada Ltd,
41 Steelcase Road West, Markham, Ontario, Canada
Penguin Books (N.Z.) Ltd,
182–190 Wairau Road, Auckland 10, New Zealand

First published 1975
Copyright © Malcolm Carrick, 1975

Made and printed in Great Britain by
Cox & Wyman Ltd, London, Reading and Fakenham
Set in Monotype Bembo

For Barny and Clair

Contents

1. Once There Was a Boy

Once there was a boy who didn't enjoy anything; the only thing he enjoyed was pulling girls' pigtails. He was an awful boy.

One day he saw a little girl walking along with her dog; she had such lovely pigtails he crept up behind her and ... yank! The little girl yelled, and started crying.

She cried so much it made her dog very unhappy; so unhappy, in fact, that he stopped chasing the cat next door, which made the cat think there was something wrong with him, and he worried too. He was so bothered about the dog not chasing him that he stopped chasing the mice. When the other cats saw the cat next door wasn't chasing mice they thought, 'Well, we'd better stop too.'

Now the mice were used to being chased; it kept them fit and healthy; so that when the cats stopped chasing them they grew listless and stopped eating so much corn in the fields. Now, as the mice used to eat mountains of corn, when it was time for the farmers to bring it into the barns, there was far too much.

Well, the farmers didn't mind, and they crammed it into the barns, which weren't used to such vast amounts of corn and barley, and couldn't stand the strain. They all burst. This meant the farmers had to leave milking the cows to pick up all the corn and barley and rebuild the barns.

Now cows can't milk themselves, and the farmers

were very busy mending the barns and so there was no milk being sent to the cities. The cities were full of people who drank lots of milk, and as there was no milk for their morning cornflakes the people had to make do with water.

Well, the water was being used up much faster than usual and soon all the rivers and lakes started drying up. The rivers and lakes were full of fish of course, and fish needed water as much as the people did. So the fish had to look for somewhere else that was wet, and that meant they all came down the rivers to the sea.

The sea is a huge place, and although there were lots of fish in the sea, all the fish from the rivers and lakes simply filled it. The fish could hardly swim for other fish, which made things very difficult for all the ships and boats.

The sea was so full of fish that the boats wouldn't float properly. So they all had to stay in the harbours, which got more and more crowded as more and more boats came in and the harbours simply couldn't hold them. So all the boats and ships were put on the roads, which soon filled the roads chock-a-block with ships. Now, obviously, the cars couldn't drive on roads full of ships, so they drove on to the railway lines, which was better until the engine drivers wanted to start the trains running.

By now there was nowhere left for the trains to go – they couldn't go on the roads because they were full of ships, and they couldn't go on the tracks because they were full of cars – so the trains had to go across country. They ploughed across the fields, which greatly disturbed the rabbits, who couldn't sleep for all the noise of overhead trains. So the rabbits took to sleeping in the trees, which was all right for them, but left nowhere for the birds to nest as all the trees were full of rabbits.

Well, the birds flew around for a bit until they found the only places left were church steeples, so all the birds built nests in the church steeples. Now steeples usually have only a few birds in them and they couldn't stand the weight of so many extra ones, so finally with a mighty clang all the church bells fell down. C L A N G!

Now there was a very shy little church mouse in one of the steeples, and he hated loud noises, so when all these bells started clanging to the ground, he jumped up and ran for his life, right up to the cat next door. The cat hadn't seen a mouse running like that since they

stopped being chased, and so he thought, 'Something's wrong, he's chasing me.'

So the cat next door ran away from the mouse, and when the little girl's dog saw the mouse chasing the cat he thought the world must be upside down, and if it was, then he had better run away from the cat.

And the sight of a mouse chasing the cat, chasing the dog, made the girl with pigtails feel better, and it made the awful boy laugh so much, he laughed and laughed . . . all his life, and of course, if you laugh all the time, when you grow up you can't shave your face. So as the boy grew older and older he laughed and laughed and couldn't shave in case he cut himself, so he grew a long, long beard.

One day, another rude boy came along and saw the laughing old man with a beard.

'Why are you laughing?' said the boy.

'Well, ha ha, I saw a mouse chasing a cat chasing a dog,' the old man laughed.

'How did that happen?' asked the boy.

'It all happened because I pulled a girl's pigtail,' the old man laughed.

'Like this?' asked the boy, and he pulled the old man's beard.

'OUCH.' The old man stopped laughing. Now when the old man had his beard pulled he realized how much it hurt, and from that day to this he never pulled anybody's pigtails – or beard.

2. The King of the Jungle

There's a lion in the jungle who goes ROAR, ROAR,
  ROAR,
and the monkeys think that he's a crashing BORE,
  BORE, BORE,
and the elephants are likely to get SORE, SORE,
  SORE,
when they hear the lion roaring with his ROAR,
  ROAR, ROAR.

'You're making too much noise, you KING, KING,
  KING.'
'Yes,' cried all the others, 'can't you SING, SING,
  SING?
'Or be quiet like the raindrops and PING, PING,
  PING?
'You really are a noisy KING, KING, KING.'

The king of the jungle said 'ROAR, ROAR,
  ROAR,'

and hit the ground with his PAW, PAW, PAW.
'I don't believe there's a LAW, LAW, LAW,
'against a king in his jungle going ROAR, ROAR,
   ROAR.'

3. The Bell Tower

Once there was a king who loved to hear the sound of distant bells.

'How calm and restful,' he would say. He liked the sound so much he decided to have his own bell tower built. So he called for his builder, and said, 'Build me a fine bell tower.'

'Right ho, Your Majesty,' said the builder, and off he set to get the bricks and cement and wood and bells to build the tower.

Well, the king sat by his window as usual, listening to the meadowlark and the distant sound of children singing, when suddenly there was a screeching, scratching noise.

'Oh, what a terrible noise,' cried the king, and he shouted to the builder, 'What's all that racket?'

'Why,' the builder answered, 'I'm sawing the wood to hold up the bell tower.'

'It's much too loud and noisy,' said the king. 'Use a quiet saw.'

'There isn't such a thing as a quiet saw, Your Majesty.'

'Well then, use paper instead of wood.'

'But . . .' the builder began, but the king wouldn't listen, so the builder went back to building the tower and the king went back to listening to the quiet restful sounds of the birds singing, and the river trickling past the palace.

But then there was a scraping noise!

'Aaarrgh! What's that horrible noise?' cried the king.

'Why, I'm mixing the cement to hold the bricks together, sire, like this,' said the builder, shovelling the cement.

'I won't have such horrid loud noises,' said the king. 'Use something quieter. Use . . . cotton wool.'

'But that won't hold the bricks together,' complained the builder.

'Oh well, put some glue on it,' said the king.

So the builder went back to building the tower, and the king went back to listening to the quiet countryside around the palace.

'I shall be glad to have nice chiming bells just outside my window,' the king thought. Just then he was interrupted by a rattling, clanging, noise.

'What's that?' the king started. 'Builder, builder, what's that dreadful noise?'

'Why,' the builder cried through the king's window, 'we're pulling up the bells with chains.'

'It's much too loud,' the king said. 'Do it with string.'

'But string won't hold up the bells, sire,' complained the poor builder.

'DO IT WITH STRING,' the king said imperiously.

So the builder went back to finish the bell tower.

Soon the tower was finished and the bells were in place. The king was very pleased. 'There you are,' he told the builder, 'there was nothing to worry about. Paper is just as good as wood, and the string is quite strong enough to hold the bells, and the cotton wool will hold the bricks.'

'Well, I don't know, Your Majesty, I don't know,' the builder said nervously.

'Start the bells ringing,' said the king, and he waved

to the bell ringers, and settled down to enjoy the sweet
sound of pealing bells.

But when the bell ringers pulled on the bell ropes,
the tower started to wobble with the weight of the

bells swinging, and with an almighty C R A S H! the bell tower fell down.

'Oh dear,' the builder said; he was covered in dust. 'I'm afraid the tower wasn't strong enough.'

'What?' asked the king.

'I said . . .' started the builder.

'I can't hear you,' the king said.

The great big crash had made the king go a bit deaf.

'Build another tower,' he said, holding his ears.

'All right,' shouted the builder, 'but I'll build it properly this time.'

And he did. And because the king's ears were still ringing from the crash, he didn't notice all the building noises. But by the time the tower was finished the king had his hearing back and was able to listen to the bells whenever he wanted to; and that tower never fell down.

4. Sounds

The bottles go poppity, poppity, pop,
The horses go cloppity, cloppity, clop,
Stones in the water go ploppity, plop,
And when I'm tired I droppity . . . drop.

The wheels go clickity, clickity, click,
The clock goes tickity, tickity, tick,
The cat eats the cream, lickity, lick,
And when it freezes I slippity,
                                    slip.

The car horn goes peepity, peepity, peep,
The birds go cheepity, cheepity, cheep,
The hares in the field go leapity, leap,
Then everything goes to sleepity, sleep.

5. Susie's Hair Ribbon

One day Susie decided to put her new pink hair ribbon in her hair. She looked around her room, but she couldn't see it anywhere.

'Oh bother,' Susie said, 'I'm always losing things!'

So she looked under her bed. She didn't find her hair ribbon, but she found the lid of her jewel box.

'I've been looking for that.' And Susie put the lid back on her jewel box.

Then she looked through all her drawers for her hair ribbon. She didn't find the pink ribbon, but she did find 5p her aunt gave her last Christmas.

'I've been looking for that,' Susie said, and put it in her money box.

Then she looked under the carpet. She didn't find her hair ribbon, but she did find the key to her wind-up train.

'Oh, I've been looking for that,' she said as she put it with the train.

Next she turned out the wastepaper basket. Susie didn't find her hair ribbon, but she did find her doll's lost shoe.

'I've been looking for that,' she said, and put it on her doll's foot.

Susie thought her new pink hair ribbon might be in her school bag, so she turned that out. She didn't find the ribbon, but she did find the pencil sharpener she thought she had lost.

'I've been looking for that,' she said and went to put it in her school bag, but as it was there already, she went on searching for her hair ribbon.

'Perhaps it's in my dolls' pram,' she thought, so she had a good rummage about in there. She didn't find the hair ribbon, but she did find the shiny medal her uncle had given her.

'I've been looking for that,' she said, and she put it in her dolls' pram so that she would know where to find it again.

The last place she could think to look was in her toy box. She turned that out on the floor, but still she didn't find her hair ribbon. But she did find a frilly piece of lace that she'd been saving.

'I've been looking for that,' she said and put it in her sewing bag. Then she rushed downstairs.

'Mum,' she yelled, 'I've found the lid of my jewel box, and the key of my train, and 5p that Aunty gave me for Christmas, and my doll's shoe and my pencil sharpener, and uncle's shiny medal, and my frilly piece of lace. But I still didn't find my new pink hair ribbon that I was looking for.'

'Well no wonder,' her Mum laughed. 'It's in your hair, Susie.'

Susie felt her hair, and there was the pink ribbon; it had been there all the time.

'I was looking for that,' she said.

6. Lost It

You know where you've seen it
But you can't think where.
Have you ever lost a sock
From your last clean pair?
You ask your big sister
But she doesn't care.
Turn out the drawers,
Look under the stair,
Behind the wardrobes,
'Oh dear, it's not there.'
Where can it have gone?
It was here in this tin.
It might have been taken!
Thrown in the bin!
Rummage about,
Now don't get so tearful.
'I bet it's my Dad
'Having a leg-pull.

'Yes, I've looked in my room,
'I've searched all around it;
'Oh, what's this here?
'Hooray, look, I've found it.'

7. David Is Lost

One sunny morning David and his Mum and Dad
arrived at their new house. David used to live in a
quiet little house, but now he was to live in the city.
It was very different: all around were tall buildings
stretching up and up and blocks of flats of people

hustling and bustling, and moving around the balconies, waving hello to each other.

David felt quite dizzy looking up at his new home in the middle of a great block of flats. He wondered if he would like it here. He didn't know anybody at all and he felt quite strange as he followed his Mum up the staircases into the lifts and along the passageways of the new flats. Even when their furniture was moved into the flat on the sixth floor and his Mum and Dad were there, he still felt a bit unhappy.

'I don't have any friends here,' he said to his Mum.

'Oh, you'll soon have some friends when you go to school, David,' Mum smiled. 'Look out of the window, you can see your school from here.' David looked out into the city.

There were miles and miles of streets and alleys and shops and people. Everywhere you looked there were people.

'All those people,' David sighed, 'and I don't know anybody.'

David went downstairs and stood at the front door to look around. There was a policeman on duty by the crossing, stopping the cars, and the caretaker of the flats was brushing the yard. Across the road the shops were open and people from the flats were going in and out. They all smiled at each other, but no one said hello to David. He went upstairs again, feeling very unhappy.

The next day David's Mum took him to his new school. It was a short bus-ride down the road.

'Now, David,' she said, 'remember when you come back, the flat is on the sixth floor.'

All day David tried to remember the number of his flat, but after all the counting at school, his head was full of numbers and when it was time to go home he had quite forgotten which number the flat was.

'Oh, dear,' he thought as he got on the bus; but he was a big boy and he knew he'd find his way home somehow.

'Where are you going?' asked the driver.

'I live along this road,' David said, 'but I've forgotten the number.'

'What! Forgotten where you live? What's your name, or have you forgotten that?'

'No, it's David.'

The driver laughed, and told David to look out of the window until he saw his flats, then the driver, whose name was Bill, would stop.

David looked at all the flats whizzing past. They were all very alike, but at last he recognized his block. Then he thought he remembered that policeman standing by the traffic lights.

'There it is, Bill,' he told the driver. 'But I still can't remember which floor I live on.'

Bill got out and took David over to the policeman.

'He's lost, Joe,' Bill the driver said to the policeman.

'Forgotten where you live!' policeman Joe said. 'Well now.'

He took out his notebook and wrote very carefully in it.

'Have you forgotten your name?' he inquired.

'Oh, no, it's David,' David replied.

'Ah, well, come on, let's look inside the flats.'

So bus-driver Bill and policeman Joe and David went across the road into the flats. There was the caretaker sweeping the yard.

'Hey, Sam, do you know where this boy lives? He's forgotten.'

'I think it's the top floor,' David said.

Caretaker Sam looked and then smiled. 'Forgot where you live! Oh, you'll forget your head, son. What's your name?'

'David,' said David, who felt a bit miserable, 'and I'm lost,' he added.

'We know that,' said the bus-driver and the policeman and the caretaker. 'Let's go up to the top floor.'

Off they all went, into the lift. And there was a priest.

'Ah, Father John,' said the policeman, 'do you know this lad? He's forgotten where he lives.'

'Oh, dear, dear, dear,' said Father John. 'What's your name, my son?'

David said 'David,' and, squeezing into the lift, added, 'I think it's on the top floor.'

So up to the top floor went the driver, the police-man, the caretaker, and the priest. They knocked on all the doors.

'Does David live here?' they asked. All the people looked at David and said hello, but nobody knew where he lived.

'I remember now, it's the bottom floor,' David said, getting very confused.

'Come on, then.'

There were too many people to get in the lift. So the bus-driver and the policeman and the caretaker and the priest and all the people on the top floor started down to the bottom floor.

When they got around the corner there was another crowd of people. They were the passengers from the bus. 'Where's the driver?' they asked.

'He's looking for David's flat,' said the policeman.

'Why?' asked all the passengers.

'Because he's lost,' said the driver, the policeman, the caretaker, the priest, and the people from the top floor.

'Oh, we'll help you,' the passengers from the bus said, and off went the procession with David at the head, down to the bottom floor. But his flat wasn't there.

The people on the bottom floor were very helpful and followed the passengers from the bus, behind the people from the top floor; behind the priest, John; behind the caretaker, Sam; behind the policeman, Joe; behind the driver, Bill; as they went upstairs again. What a procession it was. Soon all the shop-keepers from across the road came to see what was happening, and all the drivers from the cars which were waiting for the empty bus to move stopped toot-ing their horns and, shouting for the policeman, got out of their cars, and came across the road to the flats.

'What's going on? Why is there no policeman on duty?'

'We're looking for David's flat,' said the driver and the policeman and the caretaker and the priest and the top-floor people and the passengers and the bottom-floor people and the shop-keepers.

'We'll help,' agreed all the car drivers. And so everybody went knocking on doors, asking if David lived here.

There was such a racket going on that David's Mum looked out of her window.

'David,' she called, 'what are you doing?'

'Mum!!' David was so relieved. 'I was lost,' he cried, 'and the bus-driver and the policeman and the caretaker and the priest and the top-floor people, and the bus passengers and the bottom-floor people and the shop-keepers and the car drivers were looking for my flat.'

'Well, it's here on the sixth floor,' his Mum shouted down.

So the whole procession went up to the sixth floor.

'I know why I forgot which floor it was. I did so many sums at school,' David said.

Everybody laughed and laughed, and after they had

chatted with David's Mum and had a cup of tea, they all went back to their jobs, everyone talking about David.

David was glad to be home. 'But will I remember tomorrow?' he wondered.

He shouldn't have worried because next day when he came out of school, the bus-driver, Bill, and all the passengers laughed and shouted, 'This way, David,' and when he got to his flats the policeman, Joe, called over the road, 'This way, David,' and David waved hello to the shopkeepers and the car drivers who were tooting their horns, and crossed over into the flats.

'This way, David,' laughed Sam the caretaker, and going across the courtyard Father John shouted, 'The sixth floor, David,' and when he got to the sixth floor, all the people in the flats leaned out of their windows and over their balconies, and called, 'Hello, David.'

David looked around. All the flats were the same except for one with a red door, and there was his Mum!

'Look what Sam the caretaker has done for you, David,' she said. 'He has painted our door bright red so you'll never get lost again.'

David looked over the rail at all his friends. He knew everybody and everybody knew him.

'I'm glad I live here,' he said to his Mum. And his Mum was glad too, and so was everybody else.

8. Riddle

I grow green,
I turn red,
I leave my home,
To make my bed.

(a leaf)

9. Bother These Boots

One day a man came home very late, after a hard day's work.

He had bought a new pair of boots that day and they were very tight.

'Bother these boots,' he said, 'I shall be glad to get them off.' So he went to pull them off. Well, he tugged, and he pulled, and he yanked, and he heaved, but it was no good. The boots were stuck firmly on his feet.

'I can't go to bed with my boots on,' he said. 'And it's very late. I've got to get some sleep before work tomorrow.'

He sat on his bed and fretted. Then he had an idea. 'Perhaps someone is still about who will help me pull them off.' So he went to the window and looked out. It was very late, and the only person he could see was a railway porter going home from work.

'Hey,' he called, 'can you help me get my boots off?'

The railway porter was a kind man.

'Certainly,' he said, and he came in.

Well, the man sat on the bed, and the railway porter got his muscles flexed, and firmly grabbed a boot, and he tugged and pulled, and yanked and heaved, but it was no good.

'Bother these boots,' said the porter and the man. 'We need some more help,' they decided. So they went to the window to see who else was about.

'Perhaps that policeman can help,' said the man. So they called to the policeman on his beat.

They explained about the boots, and the policeman came in and asked the railway porter to hold him round the middle while he grasped the man's boots. Then they tugged and pulled; they yanked and heaved, but it was no good.

'Bother these boots,' said the policeman, the porter, and the man.

'What we need,' the policeman said, 'is more help with the pulling of these here boots.'

And the policeman went to the window and called out to two traffic wardens who were going to work early.

'Can you give us a hand here?' he asked. So the traffic wardens came in too. Then together with the policeman and the porter, they tried to pull off the man's boots.

But it was no good.

'Bother these boots,' they all said.

Now the man was very worried.

'It's nearly morning,' he said, 'and I still haven't got my boots off.'

'Now don't you worry,' the railway porter said, looking out of the window.

'There's a strong bus-driver going to work out there. I'm sure he'll help.'

So the porter went to the window, and asked the strong bus-driver if he would help.

'Surely,' said the driver, who understood the problem at once. 'I'll bring my conductor. He's only small, but he's got strong hands.'

Well, the little bus-conductor's strong hands grasped the boots, and the bus-driver held him, and the traffic warden held him, and the policeman held them, and the railway porter held him, and they all tugged and pulled and yanked and heaved.

And the boots came off, sending everyone crashing to the floor.

The man was delighted and thanked everyone very much as they said goodbye and went off to work.

'Now for some sleep,' he thought. But just as he got into bed and closed his eyes, the day dawned and his alarm clock went off.

'Bother these boots,' the man said. 'Time to get up for work.'

So he got up and yawned and put on his coat and pushed his toes into his boots. But he couldn't get his boots on.

So what did he do?... He went to work in his socks.

45

10. Boots

A boot, a boot, a soldier's boot,
Bright and clean for a smart salute.
A boot, a boot, a boot.

Boots, boots, workman's boots,
Muddy and old, they keep out the cold.
Boots, boots, boots.

A boot, a boot, a lady's boot,
Lace and strap, leather and jute.
A boot, a boot, a boot.

Boots, boots, footballer's boots,
Studs galore, to help him score,
Boots, boots, boots.

A boot, a boot, a baby's boot,
Tiny toes that look so cute.
A boot, a boot, a boot.

Boots, boots, Wellington boots,
Shiny for splashing, I think they're smashing.
Boots, boots, BOOTS.

11. Any Old Iron?

Alfie was digging about in his toy box.

'What are you looking for, Alf?' asked his Mum.

'Something to sell,' said Alfie. 'I need 10p to buy some new marbles for the big match at school tomorrow.'

'What about your old ones?'

'They're all lumpy and cracked,' Alfie replied.

Alfie's Dad came into the room.

'Who's lumpy and cracked?' he laughed, and Alfie explained about the marbles and the 10p.

Alfie's Dad thought for a moment; then he said, 'Why not take the old pram in the garden down to Charlie's scrap-metal yard; he might give you something for it?'

Alfie rushed downstairs. 'Cor, thanks Dad!' he yelled, and he dug the old pram out of the garden shed. It was a bit rusty and hard to push, but Alfie soon had it out of the garden, and was trundling it along the pavement when he saw Mr Jones, the old age pensioner from next door.

'Where are you going, Alfie?' he asked.

'To Charlie's scrap yard,' Alfie replied, 'to sell this pram for marbles.'

'Oh good, you might as well take this old kettle that's been kicking around my garden,' Mr Jones said, and he popped it into the pram.

Farther on up the road Alfie bumped into his Aunt Flo.

'Where are you going, Alfie?' she asked.

'I'm going to sell this pram at the scrap yard,' he said. 'If I ever get there.'

'Oh good, you might as well take my old stove then, dear, eh?'

'I suppose so,' Alfie mumbled.

Alfie was getting impatient waiting for his aunt to get the stove, and when she finally came out of the house with it, a voice called from over the road.

'Where you going?' It was Mr Smith the shop-keeper.

Alfie pretended not to hear, but his aunt said, 'I think Mr Smith wants a word with you, dear.'

Alfie pushed the heavy rusty pram across the road. 'I'm going to the scrap yard to . . .'

Before Alfie could finish, Mr Smith was loading a heap of old tin boxes on the pram.

'Yes,' he said, 'I heard you say to your auntie that you were going to the scrap yard; you don't mind taking these old tins, do you, Alfie?'

Alfie said, 'Yes I flipping do,' but it came out, 'No, Mr Smith!'

The pram was very much heavier now with the kettle and the stove and the boxes, but Alfie pushed on, thinking of his new marbles.

When he reached the end of the street, he passed Ernie's fruit stall.

'What'cha got there, Alfie, a tin baby?' laughed Ernie.

'Ha, ha,' Alfie said, and he told Ernie where he was going. But instantly he wished he hadn't because Ernie whipped out a rusty pair of scales and some very heavy-looking weights.

'No thanks, Ernie, every time I pass someone they keep giving me more things for the scrap yard and this pram is getting too hard to push.'

'Well,' Ernie said, 'if everyone else is giving you

presents I don't want to be left out,' and with a laugh
dumped the old pair of scales onto the sagging pram.

Alfie said nothing, as he needed his breath for the hill
he had to climb. The pram was very heavy now, with
the kettle and the stove and the tin boxes and the scales
and weights, so heavy that at the steepest part of the

hill Alfie thought he was going to have to let go of the pram.

'Help!' he yelled, and out of the bike shop came Alfie's brother, Bill, who grabbed the pram and pushed it to the top of the hill for Alfie.

'Thanks, Bill,' gasped Alfie. 'I forgot you worked here.'

'Where are you going with that lot?' asked Bill.

'To Charlie's scrap yard, but I seem to be collecting everyone's old junk.'

'Well I've got some old junk in the shop,' Bill said. 'Wait here, and I'll get it.'

'But Bill . . .' Alfie moaned, but it was too late. Bill disappeared and returned with a pile of chains and things and started fitting them into the pram.

'I'll never push that lot!' Alfie complained, but Bill only laughed.

So Alfie struggled off with the pram, with the kettle and the stove and the boxes and the scales and weights, and the chains and things, all clanking along inside.

The pram was really heavy now and Alfie's arms were nearly falling off when he finally reached Charlie's scrap yard. He sat on the ground and puffed.

'Hello there,' said Charlie. 'What's all this, Alfie?'

'Do you want to buy the pram?' he asked Charlie hopefully. 'I've pushed it miles and I need 10p for some new marbles.'

'Sorry, Alfie,' Charlie said shaking his head. 'It's only worth a couple of pence to me.'

Alfie's heart sank. All that work for 2p; that was no good. 'Oh,' he said and got up to leave.

'And,' said Charlie rooting about in the pram, '2p for the kettle, 3p for the stove, 2p for the boxes, 5p for these scales and weights, and 1p for the chains.'

'That's 15p,' Alfie yelled. 'Hurrah!'

Charlie paid Alfie the money, and he ran off to the toy shop. But when he got there he didn't know what to do with the other 5p. He could buy another pram and get some more junk to sell; but then he remembered all that pushing and shoving and his sore arms. So he brought another 5p's worth of marbles – the biggest and shiniest he could find.

12. Dump Land

In a land far away, called Dump Land,
There are streams of rainbow oil.
There are castles of cans and cardboard,
With turrets of crumpled foil.
It's a place where everyone's dirty,
And happy enough it would seem.
In Dump Land they wash with fish glue
And dry off with sour cream.
All the dustbins are empty in Dump Land,
As everyone wants the dust.
They stick it all over their windows
While they wait for their new cars to rust.
So if you happen to go to Dump Land,
Mind you dirty your ears.
Then the King will say with open arms,
'Welcome to Dump Land, three cheers.'

13. Gordon Goldfish

Once there was a goldfish called Gordon. He lived in a bowl on the sideboard of a nice warm house. Every day he swam around and around the bowl, waiting for his dinner, waiting for the water to be changed, waiting for fresh plants to be put in the bowl.

'Wait, wait, wait,' the goldfish moaned. 'That's all

I do.' Gordon couldn't remember anything but being in a bowl.

'I'd like to swim somewhere else,' he thought. 'There must be other places to swim.'

Then he remembered: when the water in his bowl was changed, Gordon was put in a jam jar by the side of a sink. From the jar he could see the water in the sink going down, down, down the plug-hole in the middle.

'That's what I'll do,' he decided. 'I'll flip myself down that hole when my water is changed.'

And that's what he did; down and down Gordon went, round and round in the narrow dark pipes.

'Oh, how adventurous!' he thought. As he turned the corner, he saw a funny creature with a big fat body and eight legs. It was a spider, although Gordon didn't know that, as he had never seen one before.

'Good morning, Eight Legs,' he cried gaily. 'When do they switch the lights on here?'

'No lights down here, mate,' the spider replied gruffly. 'It's a bit lighter farther on.'

'Oh, that's odd,' thought Gordon. 'Not to worry though, I'm having an adventure and besides it must be nearly dinner time.' So Gordon continued down the tunnel.

Soon the water started to get faster and faster and Gordon was rushing towards a tiny light which grew larger and larger until, with a swoosh, he tumbled out into a river, gasping for air and very hungry.

Gordon pushed himself to the edge of the rushing river where the water was flowing a little more slowly. There on the bank was a funny fat fellow with two enormous feet and a green face. It was a frog.

'I say, I say, you there with the big flippers on, when do we get our dinner?' Gordon inquired.

'Dinner?' croaked the frog. 'This is a river, lad, you have to get your own dinner here.'

Before he could ask any more questions, Gordon was rushed off down the river by the swirling current.

After a while he began to notice a funny taste in the water, a sharp bitter taste. It was salt. The river was nearing the sea.

'What horrid water,' choked Gordon.

'Not very nice, is it,' said a silky voice. Beside him was swimming a long thin creature with no legs at all. It was an eel.

'When will they change the water here, No Legs?' inquired the choking Gordon.

'They don't,' the eel replied shortly, 'and what's more you're heading for the sea, which isn't very nice for fish like you.'

Gordon wriggled as hard as he could trying to turn

round, but the water was moving much too fast.

'Oh,' he choked, 'I'm so hungry and salty and cold and ...' as he was complaining to himself he saw a worm dangling on a string.

'Food!' he cried and opened his mouth as wide as he could to catch it. He had just got the worm in his mouth when he felt himself being pulled up and up out of the water, and when he opened his eyes he was in a jam jar – he had been caught by a boy fishing.

Once Gordon had got over the shock he began to think, 'How nice and clean and warm it is in here; I'm sure to get some food and perhaps a nice bowl to swim in.'

Gordon got everything he wanted, and he never tried to jump into the sink when the boy changed his water. Lots of people came to see him, because he was the only goldfish ever to have been caught so near the sea.

'Well, I always was a rather adventurous fellow,' Gordon would think. 'I wonder what's for dinner.'

14. If

If I were a bear, a grizzly bear,
I wouldn't politely pull, I'd tear,
and rip and growl and grunt and scowl
and make all the squirrels stare.

If I were a bear, a brown teddy-bear,
I wouldn't just sit around in a chair,
but snuggle and huddle and comfort and cuddle
any children who might be there.

15. Doubting Thomas

Once there was a boy called Thomas, who didn't believe anything. If someone said,

'Thomas, your shoelace is undone,' he would look in the air and say,

'Nonsense, I don't believe you,' and so he was always falling over his shoelaces, and lots of other silly things too.

One day he was going to school when a huge golden lion jumped out in front of him.

'Hello, little boy, I'm an escaped lion,' he roared, expecting Thomas to die of fright.

'Nonsense,' Thomas said, walking on. 'I don't believe it.'

The lion was amazed and roared extra hard, jumping in front of Thomas again.

'Grrrrrr. I'm a lion. Aren't you scared?'

'Lions live in the zoo, not in the road,' Thomas said, looking down his nose at the roaring creature.

'But I've escaped,' the lion said. 'Honestly.'

'Oh, rubbish,' Thomas said, walking on. 'I have to go to school, excuse me.' Thomas was quite polite sometimes.

'Wait, wait,' the lion implored. 'Look, look, you just watch me frighten that policeman.'

He leapt across the road and roared at the policeman conducting the traffic, who ran away, not surprisingly shouting to everybody to run for their lives. The lion padded back to Thomas.

'There, you see, I am a lion.'

'No you're not,' Thomas said. 'The policeman was probably going home for his tea anyway.'

'What can I do to prove I'm a lion?' the lion asked Thomas.

'Well now, I once saw a lion in a circus jump through a hoop,' Thomas replied.

The lion ran off, shouting 'Come on, there's a circus at the Common. I'll show you.'

So off they went. Thomas didn't believe his friend was a lion, but he didn't want to go to school anyway.

At the circus everybody ran away from the huge lion, shouting, 'Escaped lion, run, run!'

'Run, little boy,' said the Ringmaster. 'The lion's escaped.'

'Oh, you don't believe that, do you?' Thomas laughed, and went into the big ring. There was the lion, jumping through burning hoops and growling and roaring.

'There, see,' he panted.

'I've just remembered,' Thomas told him, 'I once

saw a sea lion do that. Perhaps you are a sea lion. Can you swim?'

'NO, and I'm not a SEA LION, I'M A REAL LION, honestly.' The animal was so upset he sat down and cried. Thomas was very sorry.

'Oh, all right then,' he said, sitting down beside the poor lion. 'I'll believe you are a lion if you eat somebody.'

T—OTWB—D

'There's no one here except you.'

'Eat me, then, if you are a lion.'

'I don't want to eat you,' the lion said, very hurt. He rather liked Thomas; everybody else he tried to be friends with always ran away.

Just then the zoo catchers rushed into the big tent and surrounded them.

'Ask these zoo catchers then, Thomas; go on, ask them if I'm a lion.'

Thomas did, but the zoo men just said:

'Keep still, sonny; don't move,' and they crept closer and closer; the lion roared, ready to spring onto the men and escape again, but he suddenly stopped.

'Would you believe I was a lion if I was in the zoo?' he wondered.

'Oh yes, of course,' said Thomas.

'Then I give myself up,' the lion said to the surprised zoo keepers.

The keepers put him in a special cage and lifted him onto the zoo lorry waiting outside.

'You will come and see me, Thomas, won't you; promise?'

'All right,' Thomas said, waving goodbye. 'I

wonder if he is a lion; he certainly seems to be going to the zoo.'

So Thomas followed the van and sure enough, it went straight to the zoo; and who was in the lion's cage, but the golden lion, Thomas's friend.

'Hello, Thomas; now do you believe I'm a lion?'

'Well, yes, I suppose so,' Thomas admitted. 'You look more like a lion now.'

The lion was very pleased, and Thomas promised to visit him every day. They became very good friends, and when Thomas told his friends he had been to the circus and a zoo with a real lion, they laughed and said:

'We don't believe you, Thomas.'

In fact, nobody believed Thomas had a lion for a friend. But he did.

16. Boys

Jump Jack and Billy,
Tell Tom he's silly
And Fred's hit Willy
And Albert's chasing Joe.

Jump Mac and Bertie,
Your brother Sid's dirty
And Johnny's sister Gertie
Has trod on Peter's toe.

17. The Bridge

The squirrels were complaining again. 'It's no good,' they said in their chattering way. 'It's no good at all.'

The squirrels lived in a large wood divided by a swift stream. Some of them lived on one side of the stream and some on the other. On the bank there was only a single ash tree and if the squirrels wanted to cross the stream they had to trek for miles to a place where the trees formed an arch and the squirrels could jump from one tree to another over the stream.

'What's no good?' asked a passing beaver.

'We can't get across the stream here like you can, Beaver,' they said. 'We can't swim.'

'You need a bridge,' said Beaver.

Much to the squirrels' delight, Beaver said he would cut down the big ash tree by the stream so it would fall across it and make a bridge.

It was too big a job for one beaver, so he called some friends; but after much gnawing they had only cut out half of the tree. So they sat under the branches of the ash tree with the squirrels and looked over the stream, thinking.

'What are you squirrels and beavers thinking so hard about?' asked a badger who was passing.

'We want this tree to fall over the stream for a bridge,' said the squirrels. 'Can you help?'

Badger looked at the tree. 'Well,' he said slowly, 'if all us moles and badgers dug behind the tree and uncovered the roots, the tree would just fall down.'

So Badger got some moles and badgers and dug under the tree. They dug for hours; but even when they had a huge hole it was no good: the tree didn't fall over, it didn't even move. So the badgers and the moles sat under the tree with the beavers and the squirrels, thinking.

'What are you all thinking so hard about?' asked a passing stag.

'We want this tree to fall over the stream for a bridge,' the squirrels explained.

'Oh. Well, perhaps I could push it over with my antlers,' offered the stag, and he tried. He pushed and banged and buffeted the tree, but the tree only shook a little.

'I'm puffed,' said the stag and he leant against the ash tree with the badgers and the moles and the beavers and the squirrels, and they all sat and looked at the stream and thought.

'Whatever are you lot doing round that tree?' asked the big brown bear who was passing.

'We want to get this tree over the stream for a bridge,' they all said.

'Well,' the big bear said, blowing out his chest. 'I'll sit on a branch and weigh it down for you.'

The bear climbed up the tree and along to the end of a branch that stuck out over the stream. The branch bent a little, but the tree didn't move.

'Come on, everyone,' he called, 'help me.'

So the squirrels sat on the tree with the bear, and the stag and the beavers; and the badgers and the moles pushed hard against the trunk.

'I think ... that we're moving,' said a little squirrel on top of the tree.

'The water seems to be getting closer,' observed another squirrel half-way down.

'Whatever are you doing?' asked a robin, fluttering about looking for a place to land on the crowded branches.

The animals were just going to explain to the new arrival, when the robin sat on a branch, and his weight and the weight of the bear and the squirrels and the efforts of the stag and the badgers and the moles and the beavers were too much for the tree.

With a creeeee... CREEEEE... CREEEEEKKKKK the tree started falling.

'Jump!' the squirrels cried and they all did, just as

with an almighty CRASH the tree fell over the stream, making a perfect bridge.

'Who'd have thought a robin could weigh so much he could pull over a tree?' the squirrels wondered as they danced on their new bridge.

18. Beside the Swirling Waters

Beside the swirling waters   (*swirl fingers*)
Stood the dainty daughters.
                              (*wiggle fingers, hands apart*)
'Dad, we'll get our feet wet (*invert fingers, and wiggle*)
And we cannot swim yet.'   (*swimming action*)
Father said a bridge he'd build,   (*hammer action*)
And soon his promise was fulfilled.
                        (*slowly draw finger-tips together*)
He painted the bridge a brilliant blue (*painting action*)
And it opens up to let ships through.
                              (*resume bridge, lift hands
                              and put head through them,
                              going 'chug, chug'*)

19. Odd Socks

Mr Samuel Clerk was fed up. Every work-day he dressed in the same old way: red socks, brown suit, red woolly gloves, brown hat, brown shoes, or blue socks, blue suit, blue woolly gloves, blue hat, and black shoes, if the red and brown set needed cleaning. No-one at the office noticed him much, because he always looked the same. Mr Samuel Clerk was fed up with looking the same.

'Oh,' he yawned one Monday morning, 'I wish I could dress differently somehow or buy a new fancy suit.' But he didn't get much money at the office and couldn't afford a new suit. So Mr Clerk put on his brown clothes and went to the office.

At the office a funny thing happened. First one giggling girl, then another, came in to see him.

'What's the joke?' he asked.

'You've got odd socks on, Mr Clerk,' they giggled, and so he had.

'Oh,' he smiled, 'how silly of me.' It looked rather funny, one red sock and one blue one, but he didn't mind. 'It makes a change,' he said.

The next day, Tuesday, as he was getting dressed, Mr Samuel Clerk realized that although he had two pairs of socks, one of the red ones needed washing and so did one of the blue ones. The only clean pair he had was one red and one blue.

'Ha, ha, I'll have to wear odd socks again,' he laughed as he put on his blue suit. At the office more people came in to see Mr Samuel Clerk.

'Odd socks again eh, Samuel?' they all said. 'You are a laugh,' and they went on chatting and joking in a friendly way until at the end of the day, Mr Samuel Clerk had made a few new friends.

Now the next day, Wednesday, his first pair of odd socks had come back from the laundry and the other pair of odd socks was dirty.

'I can't wear one clean sock and one dirty sock,' he thought, 'so it's odd socks again, and if I'm wearing one red and one blue I might as well wear one part of a brown suit and one part of a blue one.'

So he put on odd socks and a blue jacket and brown trousers, and went to work.

That day lots more people came in to see what he was wearing, and they all had a good laugh, and Samuel laughed too; in fact he couldn't remember having laughed so much in his life. Even the boss remembered his name.

Now on Thursday morning he had a clean brown jacket and a pair of clean blue trousers and a clean pair of odd socks, so that's what he put on; and just for fun

he added a red woolly glove and a blue woolly glove,
which really did look odd.

At the office everyone was waiting to see what Mr
Samuel Clerk was wearing today. When he arrived
they all greeted him like a real friend and laughed and

chatted about his clothes. Mr Samuel Clerk was no longer fed up; he was very happy and very popular.

On Friday morning he decided to go completely odd. He put on an odd suit and odd socks, odd gloves and . . . odd shoes, one brown and one black, and went to work feeling very gay and happier than he'd been for years. He had a surprise at the office; instead of people saying, 'Hello, Mr Clerk,' or 'Hello, Samuel,' they all said 'Hello, Odd Socks Sam.' He had a nickname. He had always wanted one and that Friday was the happiest day of his life.

The next Monday morning his spirits fell. All his clothes had been cleaned and washed over the weekend, so there was no reason to go on wearing odd things.

'Who cares,' he cried gaily, and he put on odd socks and gloves and shoes and wore his suits odd too. And if anyone was to ask Odd Socks Sam why he wore odd clothes he would say: 'The other halves are at the cleaners,' and they were, of course.

20. Why Is It That . . . ?

Why is it that,
Some eggs are Brown
and some eggs are Cream,
and some eggs are sort of in-between?
and
Why is it that,
Some apples are Red
and some apples are Green,
and some are sort of in-between?
and
Why is it that,
Some people are Fat
and some people are Lean,
and I am sort of in-between?

21. Mrs Mungleotory's Shopping List

Mrs Mungleotory lives on a small island called Orkhebridshep. Her cottage is a long way from the village and the shops, and she can't get her own shopping because she is quite old and getting older every minute. So when Mr Firstmail the postman comes in the morning she gives him some breakfast and her shopping list, and he drops the list into the shops for them to deliver later.

Well, one day the postman Mr Firstmail called as usual.

'One letter, Mrs Mungleotory,' he said, and added, 'any shopping?'

'Yes please, postman, will you order me a half pound of lamb from the butcher?'

'Right,' said the postman and pedalled off.

Mrs Mungleotory went inside to read her letter. It was from her son, and it said that he was going to

visit her that very day with his wife and her sister and
their children, and several dogs.

'Oh, dear!' cried Mrs Mungleotory, running out
after the postman. 'There won't be enough meat to
go round.' But the postman was far down the road

and was already knocking at Farmer Clod-of-Wheat's door.

'Morning, Post!' the Farmer said. 'You've just caught me; I'm going into the village in my tractor.'

'There's your letters,' the postman replied. 'If you are going to the village would you order Mrs Mungleotory a ... a ... what was it she said? A something pound of something 'am.'

'Spam I expect, a pound of spam.'

'I expect that's it,' said the postman and pedalled off.

The farmer got out his tractor and set off for the village. Half-way along the road there was a 'chuga-chuga-plif-poof,' and his engine stopped.

'Blow me,' Farmer Clod-of-Wheat said, 'I've run out of petrol.'

Just then Policeman Plodaboot came by in his car.

'What's the matter?' he asked.

'I've run out of petrol, and I'll have to go back to the farm and get some.'

'Anything I can do?'

'Yes,' said the Farmer, 'could you order for Mrs Mungleotory a pound, or two, was it? of ram, no yam.'

'Yam,' said the policeman. 'Jam you mean, two

pounds of jam.' And off he drove to the village.

On the way into the village the observant Police-man Plodaboot noticed that a large tree trunk had fallen half-way across the road, so he took out his pencil and wrote down the tree's particulars. Then he settled down to wait for Farmer Clod-of-Wheat to arrive with his tractor.

'We can soon shift it then,' he said.

Just then the butcher's boy, Boylad, came cycling past.

'Do you want any help?' he asked.

'No thanks,' replied the policeman, as the boy rode by. 'Oh wait, though; order Mrs Mungleotory two pounds of jam.'

'Jam?' said the butcher, Mr Cutemup, when the boy delivered the order. 'We don't sell jam, he must have meant ham.'

So the butcher gave the boy two pounds of ham to deliver to Mrs Mungleotory, who was very worried because all her family had arrived, and she had nothing to feed them with.

'I'm afraid I've only got half a pound of lamb to go round, and that will take some cooking,' she told the family.

'Oh dear,' her guests said. 'We don't like lamb.'
Poor Mrs Mungleotory; she didn't know what to do.
Just then there was a knock at the door. It was the
butcher's boy.

86

'Here you are, two pounds of ham as ordered.'

'Oh,' said the surprised Mrs Mungleotory, 'what a clever village this is; everyone must have known that my guests wouldn't be fed on just half a pound of lamb, so they ordered more.'

But Mrs Mungleotory never found out how the butcher knew her guests preferred ham to lamb.

22. Action Rhyme

My eyes go blink,
my nose goes twitch,
my mouth goes BOO.
And if I were rich,
my pockets would jingle
and my hands would clap,
and I'd hide my money
behind my back.

23. Jim's Salute

Jim wanted to be a soldier. But everybody told him he was too young: his Mum and Dad told him, his teacher told him, and even Jim's friend, the soldier on duty outside the army barracks, told him, 'You're too young, Jim.'

But Jim didn't care. 'What do you have to do when you're a soldier?' he asked the guard.

'Well, now,' the soldier thought for a moment. 'Well, you have to . . . eh . . . march, and salute the Queen wherever you see her.'

'The Queen is coming to the Town Hall today,' Jim shouted as he marched off. 'I'll go and salute her.'

Jim marched down the road, chanting, 'Salute the Queen, salute the Queen . . .'

As Jim rounded the corner into the town square, he noticed that the pub there was called *Queen Victoria*.

'The Queen,' Jim said as he looked up at the sign of the pub, which showed a picture of a queen in a crown

and a white dress. Jim stood to attention and saluted.

'Whatever are you doing?' asked the people in the pub.

'I'm saluting the Queen,' Jim said sternly. 'You should always salute the Queen.'

'Well,' the people all agreed, 'yes you should.' And

they all stopped and saluted the Queen on the pub sign.

Jim marched on up the road past the shops, and past the post office when . . . Bump. One of the postmen came out and bumped into him, spilling his sack of letters on the pavement.

'Oh, dear,' said the postman as he went to pick up the letters.

Jim saluted. 'What are you doing?' asked the postman. 'Is your arm hurt?'

'No,' Jim said pointing to the stamps on the letters, 'I'm saluting the Queen, and I think you should, too.'

'Well yes, indeed,' the postman agreed, and he did. So did all the other postmen, and so did the people behind the counters, every time they sold a stamp or a postal order or anything with the Queen on it. The pub and the street outside it and the post office were full of people saluting. Jim marched on.

'Phew,' he thought, 'this saluting is very thirsty work,' and he decided to get a drink of lemonade from the supermarket. In the supermarket he took out his money . . . and saluted.

'What's the matter?' asked the Manager of the supermarket.

'I'm saluting the Queen,' Jim replied.

'But she isn't here,' the Manager said. 'She's going to the Town Hall.'

'But her picture's on the coins, too,' said Jim, 'and you should salute the Queen.'

'Well that's true, especially as she's coming here,' agreed the Manager, and he saluted. And so did the shop girls and the customers; and everybody in the town stopped and saluted every time they passed the pub or posted a letter or got out any money.

Jim marched on to the Town Hall. 'If the Queen is coming,' he thought, 'I'd better practise my salute.' So he did for hours and hours. At last a big black car came into view; it was the Queen.

The Mayor came out on the steps to greet her, and wondered where everybody else was. There were only the Mayor and Jim; everyone else in town was still saluting, and it took up so much time no one could get to the Town Hall to greet the Queen.

'Good afternoon,' said the Queen, and Jim leapt forward to salute.

But what do you think? His arm was so stiff from saluting he couldn't move it; and when he tried, it really hurt. The Queen and the Mayor were very con-

cerned about Jim's arm and took him into the Town
Hall to sit down and rest. Jim told them all about saluting and being a soldier.

'Well,' the Queen laughed, 'I don't think the guard
meant you to salute stamps and coins.'

The Mayor laughed too, but Jim didn't mind – the Queen had promised to make him a General when he grew up.

24. The Queen

The Queen waves with one hand   (*wave one hand*)
The King waves with two,   (*wave two hands*)
The Prince waves standing up   (*stand and wave*)
And I'll wave to you.   (*do so*)
I'll wave to you
If you'll wave to me,
And after we have waved away,
We'll both have tea.

25. The Great Tug-of-War

Once there was a carpenter who lived in a small village called Left Snoring. His name was Carpenter Strong. When he wasn't building houses or fixing boats in his workshop, Carpenter Strong loved tug-of-war.

'Come and have a tug-of-war with me,' he'd say to the villagers. And at first they did, and were so good, Carpenter Strong challenged the tug-of-war team from Right Snoring to a match. But the Left Snoring villagers quickly grew tired of tug-of-war, because they kept falling over. Very soon it seemed to Carpenter Strong that no-one ever wanted to play tug-of-war with him.

One sunny morning, into the village of Left Snoring came Mayor Proud of Right Snoring, and his tug-of-war team. He had come to challenge Carpenter Strong's team.

'We're better than your team,' Mayor Proud

boasted. 'We're so good, you can have the whole village in your team.'

'Poof,' Carpenter Strong said, who was too ashamed to admit he hadn't got a team. 'I'll meet you on the village green at twelve o'clock, and we'll see who is the strongest.'

Carpenter Strong quickly went round to all the villagers. 'Will you come and have a tug-of-war with Right Snoring?' he asked.

'No,' they all said, 'we're fed up with tug-of-war.'

Carpenter Strong was very upset; he'd always wanted to have a tug-of-war with Right Snoring, and beat that cocky Mayor Proud; but he couldn't do it by himself.

'Oh dear,' he thought, as he worked, glueing a long rope for the miller, 'I'll just have to tell them I can't get a team.' So he left the glued rope in the sun and went off to find Mayor Proud and the tug-of-war team from Right Snoring.

When he was gone, the miller came to collect his rope. 'Oh, I wonder why Carpenter Strong has left my rope here?' he said, and he picked it up. But as he did so, the rope stuck fast to his hand, and no

matter how much he struggled he couldn't let go
of it.

'I suppose I'll have to get someone to help me pull it
off,' he thought. So he shouted across to the baker's
shop, 'Baker Bread, will you help me get this rope
unstuck?'

'Surely,' said the baker; and he walked across to the

miller, and got hold of the rope, and yanked. They pulled, but it was no good.

'I'm sorry,' said the baker, 'I must get back to my shop.' But when he went to let go of the rope, he too was stuck fast, behind the miller.

'We'll have to get someone else to pull it,' said the miller, and they called to the blacksmith.

'We're stuck to this rope, Blacksmith, give us a pull.' The blacksmith grasped the rope and pulled and pushed, but it was no good.

'Sorry,' he said, 'I've got to go back to my black-smith's shop.' But when he went to let go of the rope, he too was stuck, behind the miller and the baker.

'Well, we'll have to go to the village green and get Carpenter Strong to undo us,' they decided. And off they went in a line.

'What's this,' called Grocer Green from his shop, 'a new dance? Wait for me, I love dancing.'

And before the others could warn him about the gluey rope, he too was stuck fast, behind the miller, the baker, and the blacksmith. Well, the line went round the corner, trailing the gluey rope, just when the Mayor of Left Snoring came out of his house.

'Who's playing tricks, leaving rope about?' he

said, and went to pick it up; and before he knew where he was, he found himself stuck to the rope and being dragged to the village green, behind the miller, the baker, the blacksmith, and the grocer.

The villagers of Right Snoring were very surprised. 'So you have got a tug-of-war team,' they said. 'Carpenter Strong told us you wouldn't come.'

'No, we're not a tug-of-war team,' complained the miller.

'Oh, I suppose you just happened to be glued to that rope,' said Mayor Proud in a nasty voice.

Well, all the men of Left Snoring were too embarrassed to say they really were glued to the rope; so they took their place behind the amazed Carpenter Strong, and waited for the other members of the team to get stuck to the rope; but they didn't.

The Right Snoring team picked up the other end, and the two teams took up the strain.

'Why aren't they sticking to the rope like us?' whispered the miller into Carpenter Strong's ear.

'Because I only glued half of the rope,' laughed the carpenter.

The tug-of-war began. The villagers of Right Snoring soon started falling over and losing their grip. But because the villagers of Left Snoring were stuck to the rope they couldn't let go; and soon, with much heaving and straining, Carpenter Strong and the villagers of Left Snoring won the tug-of-war.

Mayor Proud and his defeated team left the village, never to boast again.

'Now,' said the exhausted miller, baker, blacksmith, grocer, and Mayor, 'will you unglue us?'

'I might,' said Carpenter Strong, 'if you promise to play tug-of-war with me whenever I ask you.'

They had to agree, and the village of Left Snoring became famous for its tug-of-war team; and it also became famous because no-one in the village ever picked up a piece of rope unless it was picked up first by Carpenter Strong.

26. Riddle

I may be round,
I may be square,
in between a rip or tear.
You think you see me,
but I'm not there.
What am I?

(a hole)

27. Poor Old Joe

Joe was the smallest of the six Smith children. There were Charlie, Freda, Georgie, Christine, Paul and ... Joe.

Every time their Mum wanted them for something, she would tell Charlie, and Charlie would tell Freda, and Freda would tell Georgie,
and Georgie would tell Christine,
and Christine would tell Paul,
and Paul would have told Joe, but he always forgot, so Joe never seemed to go anywhere. He was always left out. Poor old Joe.

Well, one Saturday near Christmas, Mrs Smith decided to have a treat. 'Get your coat on, Charlie,' she said, 'and you can all go to the Saturday morning pictures.'

So Charlie said to Freda, 'We're going to the pictures.' And Freda told Georgie, 'We're going to the pictures.' And Georgie told Christine, 'We're going to the pictures.'

And Christine told Paul, 'We're going to the pictures.'
And Paul would have told Joe; but he forgot, so
when Joe came in from playing no one was there. Poor
old Joe.

When the family came back from the pictures, Mrs
Smith said, 'Oh, here you are, Joe; why didn't you
come?'

'Oh dear,' Paul gasped, 'I forgot again, I'm really sorry, Joe.'

'Well never mind, Joe,' his Mum smiled, 'I've got toad-in-the-hole for dinner.'

Well, Joe was cheered up no end by this, because toad-in-the-hole was his favourite dinner; and quite soon the house was full of lovely cooking smells.

'Charlie, dinner's ready,' called Mrs Smith.

'Freda, dinner's ready,' called Charlie.

'Georgie, dinner's ready,' called Freda.

'Christine, dinner's ready,' called Georgie.

'Paul, dinner's ready,' called Christine.

And Paul came running without telling Joe.

Well, there were so many children all grabbing for the biggest sausage that no-one noticed that Joe wasn't there; and when Joe happened to walk into the kitchen it was all gone.

'Oh, Joe,' his Mum said, 'didn't Paul tell you dinner was ready?'

'Oh, Joe,' Paul cried, 'I forgot. I'm ever so sorry.'

Poor old Joe. The others all said, 'Never mind, Joe, we're going to the fair this afternoon.'

So Joe had some beans on toast, and after that he stuck very close to Paul, just in case he forgot again.

Paul had eaten so much toad-in-the-hole that he felt a bit sleepy and went upstairs for a lie-down before the fair. So Joe did too, and when Paul got on his bed, Joe got on his. And when Paul fell asleep, Joe did too.

'Charlie, here's the money for the fair. Put your coat on, it looks like rain,' called Mrs Smith.

So Charlie said, 'Freda, we're going, put your coat on.'

And Freda said, 'Georgie, we're going, put your coat on.'

And Georgie said, 'Christine, we're going, put your coat on.'

And Christine said, 'Paul, we're going, put your coat on.'

Paul jumped out of bed, 'Now I must remember something . . . eh, I know . . . put my coat on,' and he did, and off they all went without Joe.

Joe didn't wake up till tea-time, just as the others were coming home from the fair.

'Oh, no!' Mrs Smith cried when she saw Joe on the stairs. 'Didn't Paul tell you?'

'No,' said Joe, miserably. 'I miss everything.'

'Oh, Joe,' Paul said, 'I'm so sorry.'

'Poor old Joe,' the others said. 'Never mind though,

Joe, it wasn't very good. We all got soaking wet at the fair.'

Joe didn't say anything as the others took off their wet coats. He just sat by the window. Suddenly, he noticed something in the sky. It was beginning to snow. Little sparkling bits first, then fast flurries; and soon the garden and the streets were covered in a blanket of crisp new snow.

'Oh Mum,' Charlie yelled, 'can we go out and play in the snow?'

'Yes,' said Mrs Smith, 'all of you.' But when they went to get their coats on . . .

'Oh no, my coat's wet,' cried Charlie.

'So's mine,' said Freda.

'So's mine,' said Georgie.

'So's mine,' said Christine.

'So's mine,' said Paul.

'Mine's not,' said Joe; and he put it on with a grin, and went out to play in the new snow, while the others had to sit inside and watch him running about and throwing snowballs, and making snowmen; and the only footprints in the garden were Joe's. And after that Paul's memory got much better, and the others never had to call him Poor Old Joe.

28. Huffer Puffer

Train clapping rhyme.
(Clap 1, 2, 3, 4 – speed up clapping in each verse)
Huffer puffer, puffer huffer, choo, choo, choo,
Here goes puffing train, whoo, whoo, whoo.
Start the engine turning, feel the gentle breeze
Huffing through the station, all your tickets please.

Chugga chugga chugga chugga, puffing down the line,
Round and round the wheels go, faster all the time.
Joggling all the people from end to end,
Chugging chugging chugging chugging, chugging
  round the bend.

Clickety clickety clickety clickety, going very fast.
Tickety tickety tickety tickety, trees, flying past.
Whooo o o o sh through the tunnel, hear the rails click.
Tickety tickety tickety tickety tickety tickety tick.
(Repeat last line and fade away.)

About the Author

Malcolm Carrick was born in London in 1945, and went to Beckenham Ravensbourne and Chelsea Schools of Art, then the London School of Film Technique. He worked in Adventure Playgrounds first during vacations, and later full time. He started writing for children in Playgrounds, and Playgroups, and spent some time in Playgroups and in Child Care. He writes stories and scripts for the BBC, and also writes songs. He plays various instruments, and is very interested in music for the under-fives.